Soul Food

Alison McCallion

BookLeaf
Publishing

Presentation by *BookLeaf Publishing*

Web: www.bookleafpub.com

E-mail: info@bookleafpub.com

ISBN: 9789357441902

First edition 2023

ACKNOWLEDGEMENT

I would like to thank my family and friends who give me encouragement and keep me going. A special mention to Andy, my husband for putting up with me jotting down ideas at bedtime and stealing the laptop! Also for encouraging me even when he doesn't realise it. To Carly for always being an encouragement and pointing me in the direction of creating a book. To Lynn for her constant help in proof reading and guiding in her godly ways. To Richard and his sermons which are often a point of inspiration. Lastly but most importantly thanks be to God for his indescribable gift. (2Cor9:15)

PREFACE

I have chosen to write on the topic of "soul food" as in these days in 2023, we need nothing more than to feed our souls. Not our stomachs. Not our bank balances. Not our mouths. Not ourselves. Not our bodies. Not our education. Not our jobs. Not our image. Not our social media, BUT our souls. All else listed is temporary. Our souls are eternal.

Life Changer

A very personal testimony.

Seven years ago, something happened, a story I want to tell
I'd been in and out of hospital, I wasn't very well
I'd just had my third baby and I'd lost a lot of blood
Honestly, I'm not joking, it was like a flood

It was touch and go for certain, I thought I'd drawn my last breath
I was sure that I was closer, closer to my death
The midwives they were marvellous, they always held my hand
To reassure me gently, that things would work out grand

I remember being rushed to theatre, and they tried to call my husband
It was 5 o'clock in the morning, this theatre trip wasn't planned!
They said they'd send a policeman to the front door to ring the bell
It crossed my mind if he answered, he'd think he was in hell

It seemed I was out forever, the midwife I heard her say
I'll tell him that you love him, and for you I'm going to pray
Now I don't know to this day, if she said that prayer you see
But I've a feeling that she did, 'cos that morning God reached to me

He began a work in me that I didn't even know
He got me thinking about afterlife, and wondering where we go
See my husband's hell, was hell at the time, the thought of losing his wife
Though we know a real hell exists where you could spend your eternal life

Thankfully I'm not heading there, I've got surety above
God chose to speak to me, and has showered me with His love
He's given us three children, he's given us our health
And He's given us our riches, in heaven, our true wealth

So, to all the staff at Causeway Hospital, I owe to you a lot
But to God I owe my life, for all my sins he's bought
He didn't let me die back then, He wasn't finished yet
He's been with me ever since, and all my needs He has met

A Sign of the Times

A prayer for hurting families

Lord it's hard these days
They say it's the sign of the times
Stabbings, riots, beatings
Everyday we hear these crimes

It's heart-breaking for these families
They have to say goodbye
To loved ones once held dearly
Forever asking why

We know that you're a Sovereign God
And for this we thank you so
Please bring us closer to you Father
Through these afflictions, help us grow

We pray your mercy on us Lord
We know your Kingdom will come
It seems this world has gone mad
Please Lord send your Son

Please bless the families hurt in trial
Surround them with your love
Extend to them your peace and comfort
Through your spirit from above

Testing

A testing time?

In the test that you're facing daily
Put your armour on and say
"Thank you Lord for Jesus
With Him I will not stray"

Everyday might be a struggle
In the world we live in right now
But we don't have to struggle alone
Testing beyond strength, God won't allow

He will provide a way out
So that we may be able to endure
The pain and testing we're going through
Our faith He's allowing to mature

For we've been called to live in freedom
To stand firm and stand up for Christ
So put the full armour of God on
And be sure Jesus paid the full price

It Won't Last Forever

5

Hopeless or not coping?

I'm not sure about you, how do you cope?
What are your methods of stirring up hope?
Do you plan each hour, each day, each week?
Or have you left it all at Jesus' feet?

I for one know it's the only way
Give up the planning, take each day
One day at a time is all you can do
Tomorrow's not promised to me nor to you

Rest assured you're never alone in this world
God's everywhere, and he takes a good hold
To those who believe in his wonderful ways
He will be with you, through all your days.

Pain won't last forever that is for sure
God has said so, and has sent us His cure
In Jesus His son who died, rose and lives
So we can live too, in the salvation He gives

If there's just one thing you remember this day
It takes only a minute to kneel down and pray
Christ offers eternal life through his blood on the cross
Don't deny Him! Don't remain lost!

Well-spring

A prayer-poem to the Lord.

Cleanse my heart Lord, cleanse my heart, of all you don't wish to see
Make it white as snow Lord, so I can clearly see Thee

Fill my heart Lord, fill my heart, with all things from above
So that I can show to others, the magnitude of Your love

Feed my heart Lord, feed my heart, like a weaned child I long for more
You never cease to amaze me Lord, with the things you have in store

Content my heart Lord, content my heart, with the life that I've been given
Keep my eyes from wandering, fix them straight to heaven

Guard my heart Lord, guard my heart, from the evils of this world
Give me the strength to make a stand, as more evil is unfurled

Still my heart Lord, still my heart, from the rush of these busy days
Draw close to me at noon and night, and listen as I pray

Ignite my heart Lord, ignite my heart, for it's the well-spring of my soul
Without it I am nothing, and without You I'm not whole

Focus my heart Lord, focus my heart, on You and on Your Word
Close out all distractions, and let Your voice be heard

Give me a serving heart Lord, one that hears Your call
Make me more like Jesus, help me give my all

Thank you Lord, oh thank you, for all you've done for me
I once was blind, a slave to sin and now completely free

I want to run the race Lord, the best that I can do
Grant me the grace to finish Lord, and all glory be to You

The Thought of Losing You

A plea for anyone I know, and all.

The thought of losing you, I find it hard to bear
It's hard to imagine Heaven without you being there
For those who're in Christ Jesus, Heaven is their home
A house is being prepared there, that they'll one day call their own

I have a fear inside me that you'll be forever lost
If only you believed that Jesus paid the cost
The bill that we should owe is that which He wiped clean
He came to earth, lived, died and rose so we can be seen…
As righteous in the eyes of God, the Maker of all things
And live these days on earth in the joy and hope He brings

Now to most it seems quite morbid, to talk of life and death
But IT IS the be all and end all, who gives you your next breath?
It comes from God in Heaven, the Maker of all things
Who carries us to safety upon His eagles' wings
So trust in Him today if it's the last thing that you do
He'll change you day by day, giving light and life anew.

Don't leave it one day longer, that could be too late
Turn to Him today, please don't say you'll wait
I regret not turning sooner, but that was all God's plan
Maybe today is YOUR day, to give Him all you can

Died to Live

Christ lives on today and forever

He died, He died, He died for me
He died at Calvary on a tree
He died, He died, He died for you
He died for Gentile and for Jew

He rose, He rose, He rose indeed
The Lord, He rose and intercedes
He rose, He rose, He is not dead
The Lord, He rose, as the Father had said

He lives, He lives, He lives today
He lives so we might find our way
He lives, He lives, He lives forever
He lives in completion of His endeavour

Don't You Worry

Do not fear about anything.

Don't you worry, don't you worry, God has it in his hand
From the hour you go to sleep and rise, everything is planned
He's got the finer detail – that sometimes blows my mind
To think He cares for one like me, the lost he came to find

The world it seems has thrown Him out, like rubbish to the bin
Some just cannot fathom, that they're deeply steeped in sin
How true the words were written; I was blind but now I see
It's what I hope for, for my friends and all my family

I pray and pray and pray again, that they might see the light
I wonder why they're stubborn, they put up such a fight
But it's not for me to say, the week, the day, the hour
God's timing is perfection, and His perfection is seen afar

God knows every one of us, deep down within our hearts
God's love for both you and me, from it we cannot part
So, take that leap of faith, God's got you in His hand
From the hour you go to sleep and rise, everything is planned

You'll find some days of sorrow mixed with those of joy
It won't be all that easy, things to you will still annoy
But you'll be sure of life eternal through Jesus Christ the King
And even with the sorrow and pain, His praises you'll still sing

Glory by Grace

Finding contentment in a discontent world.

Are you broken, sad, discontent
Unsure as to what you are missing?
Are you empty from the depths of your heart
Just needing someone to listen?

Turn around and seek Jesus
He's right there in your time of despair
He is near to the broken-hearted
And He'll show you how much he cares

If you're on the side of Jesus
You'll have medicine for your soul
No matter your life's circumstances
You can rest in the Lord and be whole

Jesus your saviour, God your hope
Nothing will ever compare
Sorrow and pain may ebb and flow
But of love, God has plenty to share

Follow in godliness, love and patience
Fight the good fight of faith
Remember whose army you're in
When you're called up to glory by grace

Our Everything

He is everything, without Him, nothing

Jesus you are our everything
From earth to heaven let us sing
Your praises, for You deserve them so
In all situations from high to low

Our troubles make our hearts grow sore
But we know we are guilty to the core
Your blood covered us, all our sins
You've given us life eternal in heaven

Thank you Lord for what you've done
Giving your one and only son
To die upon a cross so we
Could come to heaven and live with thee

It's precious Lord, your love so deep
It calms us when we cannot sleep
It softens each heart that once was hard
For this Lord, we are truly glad

We Lord Jesus cannot wait
To come across the pearly gate
That you will open and let us in
To live with you Lord, free from sin

Yesterday

Live in today

Yesterday has been
Yesterday has gone
Yesterday is in the past
Right where it belongs

Today is where we live
Today is here and now
Today is full of grace
And tomorrow if God allows

Live in peace
Live in harmony
Live in togetherness
Live in today not tomorrow

Cornerstone

For those who I know, but not very well

I don't know you well but well enough
To know that you need a saviour
Everyone does, even the best of us
A saviour to redeem all our failures

Your middle name, your date of birth
They're both a mystery
But not a mystery to the One True God
Who died for you and me

I don't know Him well enough
But I know I need Him as saviour
Everyone does even the best of us
A saviour to redeem all our failures

I see you as a friend and I care for you
Which is why I want you to know
Jesus cares for you more than I ever could
And in faith He wants you to grow

Take a look around and wonder at
The magnificence of His creation
The mountains, the sea and all in-between
Were made by His instruction

I long for your eyes to be opened
Like mine were not long ago
To see for the first time your maker
And in faith you begin to grow

I'd only be too happy
To help you along the way
I've prayed for you for some time now
In the future I'll continue to pray

I'd love to hear you've seen the light
That you've been saved by grace alone
Through faith alone in Christ alone
Having Him as your cornerstone

The happiness beaming across my face
And the angels singing with joy
Christ beside you all the way 'cause
The Lamb's book of life you've just joined

Everyday

He's in the everyday

Everyday I'm older
Everyday I'm more frail
Everyday I'm weaker
Everyday I fail

Everyday He holds me
Everyday He cares
Everyday I fail Him
Even though He's there

Everyday He warns me
Everyday He shows
Everyday I fail Him
Everyday He knows

Everyday is mercy
Everyday is grace
One day I will see Him
See Him face to face

Oh I Hope One Day You'll See

The hope I have of glory one day

If I go I'll go to glory
If I'm gone, that's where I'll be
With the Lord, at peace and joyful
Oh I hope one day you'll see

He created the earth and heaven
And all that lies between
Before a foetus or baby born
You too were created by God, and seen

He longs for us to love him so
To follow him to the end
And when we put Him first in life
On no one else you need depend

If I go I'll go to glory
If I'm gone, that's where I'll be
With the Lord, at peace and joyful
Oh I hope one day you'll see

Goodbye

A goodbye soon after my good friend Stef passed away

I tried to pen a letter about how I'd say goodbye
The tears they filled my eyes, could do nothing but cry
I prayed and prayed and prayed some more, God what can I do
A verse had come to mind and it was sent down just for you

I shared this verse with you on the last day of your life
I hope it went deep in your heart, in the middle of your strife
I wish I'd sent it sooner, to give you some more time
I wish I'd seen you more, and gave you more of mine

I hope so much you're with the angels, dancing on the gold
I hope the Lord himself has taken a strong hold
I hope to meet you once again in the heavens up above
I hope your pain is gone and all you feel is love

We maybe didn't meet up as much as we had hoped
How you've dealt with the past few years, how you've coped
Is beyond my comprehension, I'll forever be in awe
Of how you muddled on, with circumstances so raw

I'll remember all the good times and the funny ones at that
The beach walks in the freezing cold, sporting our new hats
The sharing of the houses, the ships that passed at night
And of course the smallest issue, the issue of your height

I will never forget you, not now and not tomorrow
I'll say goodbye today and get swallowed up in sorrow
That won't last forever though, because you taught me so
Don't let anything get you down, just get up and go.

So that's exactly what I'll do, Ill stumble and I'll fall
I'll jump back up and start again, just like you stand tall ;-)
You've touched so many lives, and for this I am so grateful
Friend, daughter, wife, mum, sister, you've left big shoes to fill

The verse I shared with my dear friend in the last hours of her
life was this from Romans chapter 10 verse 13 "For everyone
who calls on the name of the Lord will be saved"

I Wish

I wish I hadn't missed opportunities to share the gospel....

I wish I had spent more time, with those no longer here
I wish I had gone to visit them and held them very near
I wish I had been able, to open up Your word
To guide them in Your light and keep them in Your herd

I wish I could have been the one to be there when they needed
A shining light, a blessing, with a gospel well worth heeding
I wish that I could've been bolder with words of Jesus Christ
To tell them that He paid it all, the ultimate sacrifice

I know God promises to keep us and complete the work begun
And the first and most important step is to repent of all our sin
We do not have to carry this burden of hurt and pain
God will draw near to us and He will take the reigns

See if you trust in God and put your hope and faith in Him
You'll not be disappointed when you feel His love within
Do I wish I could spend more time with those no longer here?
Yes of course I do, and I'd hold them very near
But my hope is in my Father in Heaven who sees and hears all things
And wishes don't compare to the comfort that He brings

Note to Self

I need constant reminding to seek God first

Seek Him first in all you do
He will make a way for you
Seek Him first in all you say
He'll stay with you night and day
Seek Him first in all you think
Maybe He's your missing link?

The reason why your day's gone bad
The reason you're so easily sad
The reason work is getting you down
The reason why your children frown
The reason you don't feel Him near
The reason you begin to fear

Seek Him first in all you do
Seek Him first in all you say
Seek Him first in all you think
Maybe God's your missing link?

Born to Die

22

The simplicity of the gospel

Born of a virgin
Such divinity
Born in a stable
Humility

Sent for our sins
How incredible
Sent by the Father
Indescribable

Died to give us life
How magnificent
Rose to give us hope
Accomplishment

9 789357 441902